Busy Ant Maths

2nd EDITION

Activity Book 1B

Date: _____

Racing orders

Order numbers to 20

Teacher's notes

Children write the numbers shown on the cars on the flags, in order, smallest to largest.

Odd Jobs and Even Stevens

Identify odd and even numbers to 20

Date: _____

You will need:
- red and blue coloured pencils

| 0 | 1 | 2 | 3 | 4 | 5 | 6 | 7 | 8 | 9 | 10 | 11 | 12 | 13 | 14 | 15 | 16 | 17 | 18 | 19 | 20 |

Teacher's notes

On the number track children draw jumps of 2, starting from 0, in blue to show even numbers to 20; and jumps of 2, starting from 1, in red to show odd numbers to 20. They colour the "Even Stevens" team kit in blue and the "Odd Jobs" team kit in red.

3

Scarf sequences

Make repeating patterns

Date: _____

You will need:
- coloured pencils

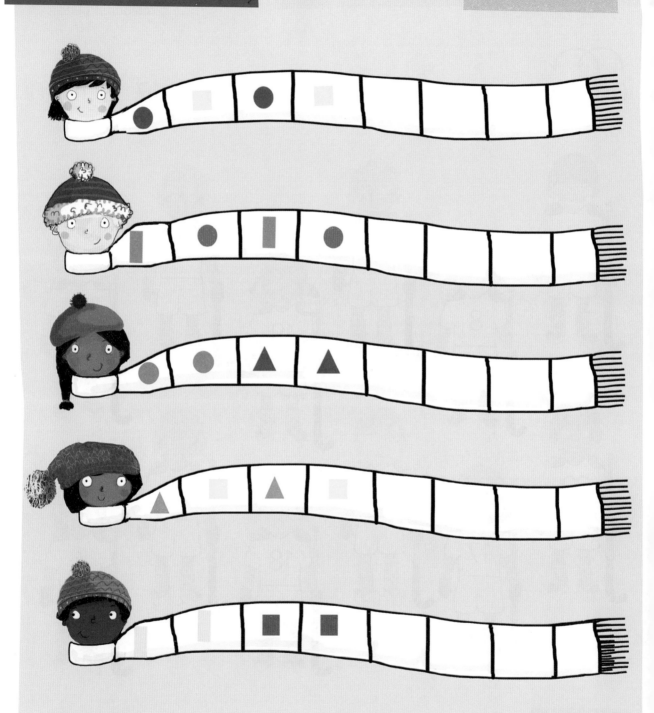

Teacher's notes

Children continue each pattern by drawing and colouring the next four shapes on each scarf.

Picture patterns

Make repeating patterns

Date: _____

You will need:
- coloured pencils

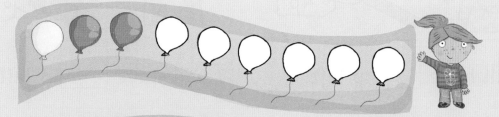

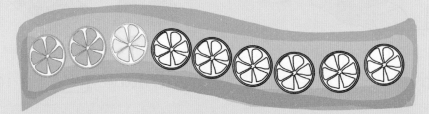

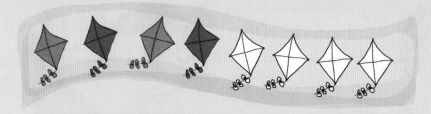

Pocket money spending

Solve problems involving money

You will need:
- some 1p, 2p, 5p and 10p coins

Date: _____

I have 6p.

4p

I will have ☐ p left.

I have 8p.

7p

I will have ☐ p left.

I have 7p.

3p

I will have ☐ p left.

I have 9p.

6p

I will have ☐ p left.

I have 10p.

5p

I will have ☐ p left.

I have 10p.

7p

I will have ☐ p left.

Teacher's notes

Children compare the amount of money each child has with the cost of the item. They work out how much money they will have left after paying. They can use coins to support their working.

Fruit stall sales

Solve problems involving money

Date: _____

bananas 5p each | pears 6p each | apples 3p each | strawberries 2p each | oranges 4p each

   2p + 3p = ☐ p

     ☐ + ☐ = ☐

     ☐ + ☐ = ☐

     ☐ + ☐ = ☐

     ☐ + ☐ = ☐

     ☐ + ☐ = ☐

Teacher's notes

For each row, children complete the addition calculation to find the total cost of the two fruits shown.

7

Date: _____

Pocket money spending

Solve problems involving money

Amber has bought:

How much has she spent?

☐ + ☐ = ☐

Tad has bought:

How much has he spent?

☐ + ☐ = ☐

Yee has bought:

How much has she spent?

☐ + ☐ = ☐

Rob has bought:

How much has he spent?

☐ + ☐ = ☐

Teacher's notes

Children work out the total for each character, then circle a combination of coins that they can use to pay exactly.

8

Date: _____

Subtraction sweet shop

Solve problems involving money

Holly has 15p.
She buys:

☐ − ☐ = ☐

How much does she have left?

Dan has 15p.
He buys:

☐ − ☐ = ☐

How much does he have left?

Imran has 15p.
He buys:

☐ − ☐ = ☐

How much does he have left?

Maya has 15p.
She buys:

☐ − ☐ = ☐

How much does she have left?

Teacher's notes

Children work out the change each character gets and complete the subtraction calculation.
Then they circle a combination of coins that might make up their change.

3-D shape names

Date: _____

Name 3-D shapes

cylinder

pyramid

cube

sphere

cuboid

cone

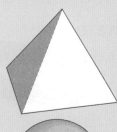

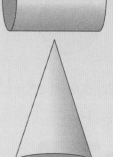

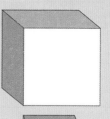

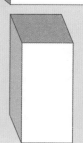

Teacher's notes

Children use a different coloured pencil to join each shape to its correct name. Then they use the same coloured pencil to colour each pair of matching shapes.

Date: _____

3-D shapes

Recognise and name 3-D shapes

You will need:
• coloured pencils

spheres cubes cylinders cuboids cones pyramids

Teacher's notes

Children help the ants to sort the shapes by colouring all the examples of each shape the same colour as the shape at the top of the page. Then they draw a line to lead each ant to all the examples of their shape, through their shape name and into the correct hole in the log.

11

Maisie's presents

Recognise cubes and cuboids

Date: _____

There are ☐ cubes and ☐ cuboids.

12

Date: _____

2-D or 3-D?

Recognise 2-D and 3-D shapes

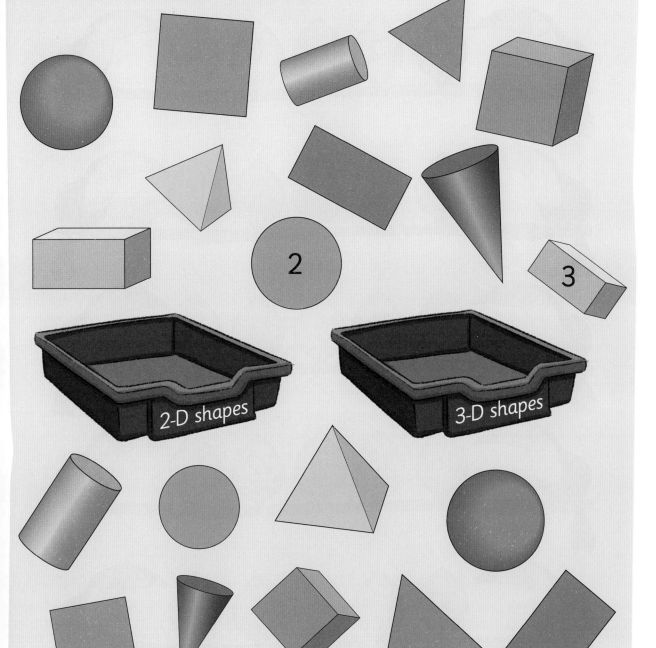

Teacher's notes

Children write a 2 on each 2-D shape and a 3 on each 3-D shape.

13

Toucan 2s

Count in 2s

Date: _____

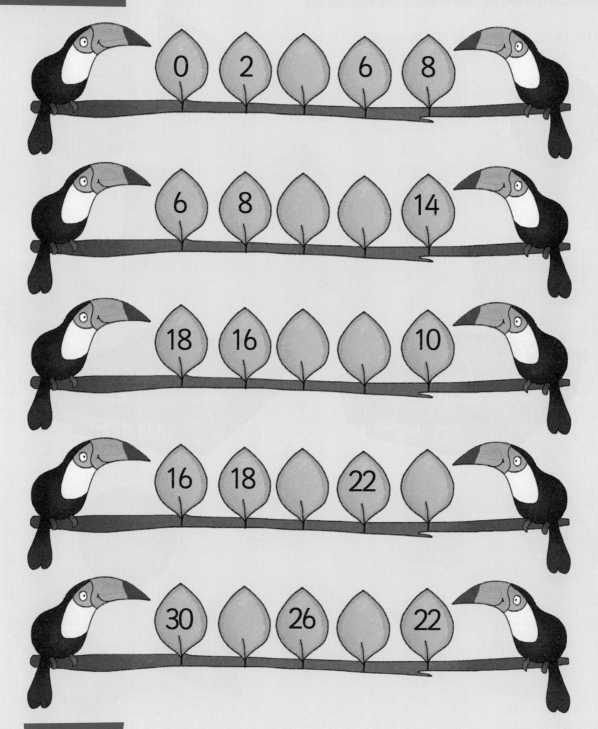

Teacher's notes

In each row, children count on or back in twos and write the missing numbers in the spaces provided.

Date: _____

Fearsome 5s!

Count in 5s

 0  5   15

 10    25

  20  25

 25    40

 35    50

Teacher's notes

In each row, children count in fives and write the missing numbers in the spaces provided.

15

Tenpin 10s

Count in 10s

Date: _____

 0

 10

 30

 50

 40

 60

 70

 90

 70

 100

Teacher's notes

In each row, children count in tens and write the missing numbers in the spaces provided.

16

Date: _____

Rows of roses

Use arrays to count in 2s, 5s and 10s

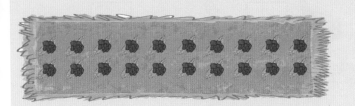

There are ☐ roses altogether.

There are ☐ roses altogether.

There are ☐ roses altogether.

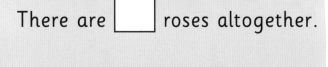

There are ☐ roses altogether.

There are ☐ roses altogether.

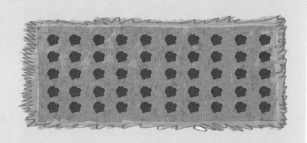

There are ☐ roses altogether.

Teacher's notes

Children draw a ring around each group of two, five or ten roses and count in twos, fives or tens to find out how many roses there are in each garden.

Lots of bugs

Date: _____

Find a total by counting groups of 2, 5 or 10

☐ groups of ☐ equals

☐ altogether.

_____

☐ groups of ☐ equals

☐ altogether.

_____

☐ groups of ☐ equals

☐ altogether.

_____

☐ groups of ☐ equals

☐ altogether.

_____

☐ groups of ☐ equals

☐ altogether.

Teacher's notes

Children count in twos, fives or tens to find out how many bugs there are on each group of leaves, and complete the sentence.

Date: _____

Solving supermarket problems

Find a total by counting groups of 2, 5 or 10

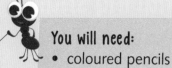

You will need:
- coloured pencils

There are 2 gloves in a pair.

Yee buys ☐ pairs.

Yee buys ☐ gloves altogether.

There are 5 oranges in a pack.

Jack buys ☐ packs.

Jack buys ☐ oranges altogether.

There are 10 stickers in a pack.

Handa buys ☐ packs.

Handa buys ☐ stickers altogether.

Now make up your own problem about groups of 2, 5 or 10.

Teacher's notes

Children count the number of groups of 2, 5 or 10 to find out how many of each item the characters buy. Then they make up their own problem about groups of 2, 5 or 10.

Sharing snails

Share objects into equal groups

Date: _____

☐ shared equally between

☐ is equal to ☐ .

☐ shared equally between

☐ is equal to ☐ .

☐ shared equally between

☐ is equal to ☐ .

☐ shared equally between

☐ is equal to ☐ .

Teacher's notes

Children count the number of snails and share them equally between the leaves by drawing them on. Then they complete the sharing sentence underneath.

Date: _____

Sharing shopping

Solve problems involving sharing

You will need:
- counting objects, such as counters or beads

Aaron has bought ☐ cakes.

He shares them equally with 3 friends.

They have ☐ cakes each.

Sarai has bought ☐ strawberries.

She shares them equally with her 2 cousins.

They have ☐ strawberries each.

Amber has bought ☐ sweets.

She shares them equally with Laura.

They have ☐ sweets each.

Ethan has bought ☐ bananas.

He shares them equally with 3 friends.

They have ☐ bananas each.

Teacher's notes

Children count the number of objects and share them equally between the people shown, using counting objects to help if needed. They write the total number of objects and the number each person gets in the spaces.

Lighter or heavier?

Date: _____

Compare weights

lighter	heavier

  |

  |

  |

heaviest	lightest

Teacher's notes

At the top of the page, children circle the lighter or heavier objects. At the bottom, they draw lines to show the lightest and heaviest objects.

22

Date: _____

Comparing mass

Understand what a balance shows

| heavier | | lighter |

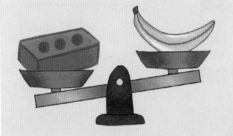

The brick is _____ than the banana.

The feather is _____ than the egg.

The football is _____ than the balloon.

The apple is _____ than the pineapple.

Teacher's notes

Children complete each sentence by writing 'heavier' or 'lighter'.

Date: _____

How many to balance?

Weigh objects

You will need:
- balance
- objects to weigh
- set of cubes, bricks or blocks

scissors [ ]

glue [ ]

toy car [ ]

2 pens [ ]

book [ ]

[ ]

your own choice of object [ ]

The heaviest object is the _____ .

The lightest object is the _____ .

2 pens weigh [ ] , so 4 pens weigh [ ] .

Teacher's notes

Children use a balance and uniform cubes, bricks or blocks to find the weight of each object and record it in the box. Then they draw a picture of their own chosen object, find the weight of it and record it in the box. Then they complete the sentences at the bottom of the page.

Date: _____

Reading scales

Weigh objects

pineapple

☐ kilogram

book

☐ kilograms

bowling ball

☐ kilograms

cat

☐ kilograms

parcel

☐ kilograms

melon

☐ kilograms

The heaviest object is the _____ .

The lightest object is the _____ .

Teacher's notes

Children write how many kilograms each object weighs. Then they complete the sentences.

25

Date: _____

Scooter route 10s

Recall pairs of numbers that total 10

You will need:
- coloured pencils

0	1	2	3	4	5	6	7	8	9	10

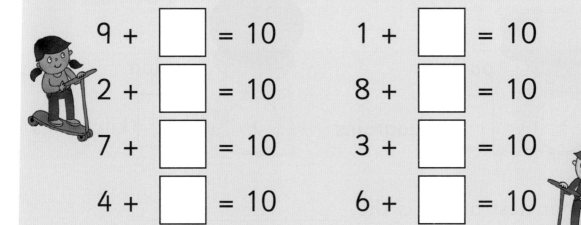

$9 + \square = 10$

$2 + \square = 10$

$7 + \square = 10$

$4 + \square = 10$

$5 + \square = 10$

$1 + \square = 10$

$8 + \square = 10$

$3 + \square = 10$

$6 + \square = 10$

$10 + \square = 10$

Teacher's notes

Children colour the addition facts that total 10 and this will then show the characters' route to the scooter park. Then they use the number track to help them fill in the missing number for each addition fact for 10.

Date: _____

Candle calculations

Use doubles to work out other addition facts

1 + 2

2 + 3

3 + 4

4 + 5

5 + 6

3+3+1

2+2+1

4+4+1

1+1+1

5+5+1

Football facts

Date: _____

- Recall addition facts within 10
- Use addition facts to find subtraction facts

You will need:
- coloured pencils

| 6 | 7 | 8 | 9 | 10 |

| 3+4 | 7+2 | 6+4 | 1+5 | 3+5 |

10 − 4 = 6   7 − 4 = 3   9 − 2 = 7

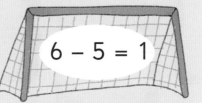

8 − 5 = 3   6 − 5 = 1

Teacher's notes

Children colour the players' tops to match the football showing the answer to their addition calculation. Then they draw a line to match each player to the goal showing the related subtraction fact.

28

Date: _____

Subtraction skateboards

- Recall subtraction facts within 10
- Use subtraction facts to find addition facts

You will need:
- coloured pencils

$6 - 3$ $7 - 5$ $8 - 4$ $9 - 8$ $10 - 5$

4   5   3   1   2

$2 + 5 = \boxed{}$ $5 + 5 = \boxed{}$

$4 + 4 = \boxed{}$ $3 + 3 = \boxed{}$

$1 + 8 = \boxed{}$

Teacher's notes

Children match the sticker showing the subtraction calculation to the correct answer by colouring the skater's top the same colour. Then they complete the addition calculations on the skateboards and colour each one to match the related subtraction.

Alien addition

Date: _____

Understand addition as counting on

0 1 2 3 4 5 6 7 8 9 10 11 12 13 14 15

3   8   ☐ + ☐ = ☐

2   10   ☐ + ☐ = ☐

5   7   ☐ + ☐ = ☐

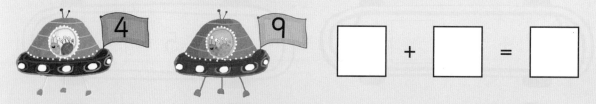

4   9   ☐ + ☐ = ☐

8   6   ☐ + ☐ = ☐

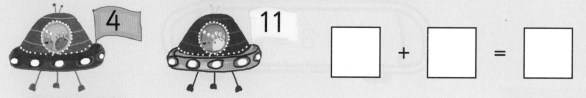

4   11   ☐ + ☐ = ☐

Teacher's notes

Children use the numbers on each pair of spacecraft to write an addition calculation. Then they complete the calculation using the number track if needed.

Snail trail subtraction

Date: _____

Use a number track to take away

0 1 2 3 4 5 6 7 8 9 10 11 12 13 14 15

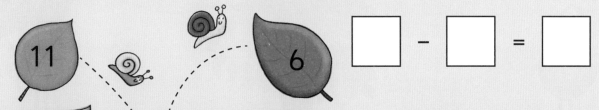

11   6   ☐ − ☐ = ☐

12   7   ☐ − ☐ = ☐

13   8   11 − 8 = ☐

14   9   ☐ − ☐ = ☐

15   10   ☐ − ☐ = ☐

☐ − ☐ = ☐   ☐ − ☐ = ☐

Teacher's notes

Children trace over each snail trail from left to right, e.g. from 11 to 8, then write the subtraction calculation and answer. At the bottom of the page they draw two different snail trails, e.g. 11 to 7, and write the subtraction calculations in the spaces provided.

Missing mangoes

Date: _____

Solve addition and subtraction missing number problems

0 1 2 3 4 5 6 7 8 9 10 11 12 13 14 15

$11 + \boxed{} = 15$

$12 - \boxed{} = 5$

$14 - \boxed{} = 8$

$3 + \boxed{} = 12$

$5 + \boxed{} = 14$

$15 - \boxed{} = 7$

Teacher's notes

Children use the number track to count on or back to find the missing number in each addition or subtraction calculation.

Date: _____

Pirate treasure patterns

Recognise patterns in addition and subtraction facts

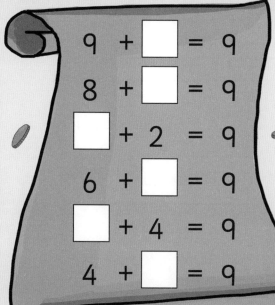

9 + ☐ = 9
8 + ☐ = 9
☐ + 2 = 9
6 + ☐ = 9
☐ + 4 = 9
4 + ☐ = 9

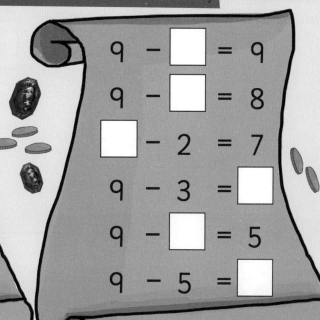

9 − ☐ = 9
9 − ☐ = 8
☐ − 2 = 7
9 − 3 = ☐
9 − ☐ = 5
9 − 5 = ☐

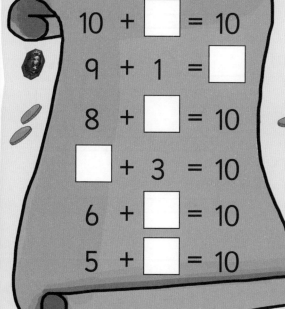

10 + ☐ = 10
9 + 1 = ☐
8 + ☐ = 10
☐ + 3 = 10
6 + ☐ = 10
5 + ☐ = 10

10 − ☐ = 10
10 − ☐ = 9
☐ − 2 = 8
10 − ☐ = 7
10 − ☐ = 6
10 − 5 = ☐

Teacher's notes

Children work out the missing number in each calculation, using the pattern of addition or subtraction to help.

Days and months

Order the days of the week and months of the year

Sunday	→	

	Wednesday

November		March

	June

Teacher's notes

Children write the missing days of the week in the spaces provided at the top of the page.
Then they write the missing months of the year in the spaces provided at the bottom of the page.

Sequencing events

Put events in order

Date: _____

 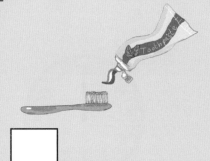 

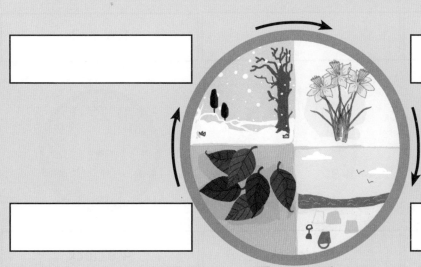

O'clock

Read and show o'clock times

Date: _____

| 2 o'clock |

| |

| |

| |

| |

| 1 o'clock |

| 6 o'clock |

| 9 o'clock |

| 4 o'clock |

Teacher's notes

Children write the time underneath each clock face or draw hands on the clock face to show the time given.

Half past

Read and show half-past times

Date: _____

half past 2		

		half past 3

half past 5	half past 11	half past 8

Teacher's notes

Children write the time underneath each clock face or draw hands on the clock face to show the time given.

Name that number!

Write numbers in numerals and words

Date: _____

1 | one

2

3

4

5

6

7

8

9

10

Teacher's notes

Children write the number names in the spaces provided.

Date: _____

Place value races

Find the number of 10s and 1s in numbers to 20

1 ten and 4 ones

1 ten and 3 ones

1 ten and 2 ones

1 ten and 6 ones

1 ten and 5 ones

1 ten and 9 ones

1 ten and 7 ones

2 tens

Teacher's notes

Children use the number of tens and ones to work out each racing car's number and write it on the side of the car.

Counting and ordering to 20

Compare and order numbers

Date: _____

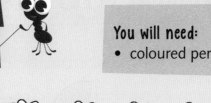

You will need:
• coloured pencils

• 1 more than 10

• 1 less than 20

• 1 more than 6

• 1 less than 14

• more than 5 but less than 10

• more than 10 but less than 20

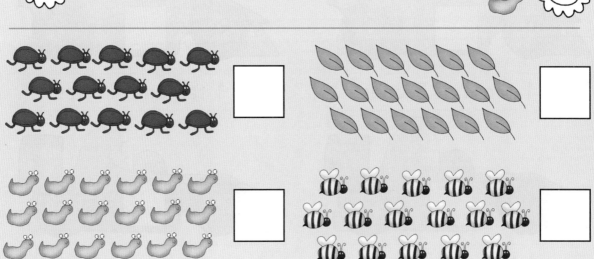

40

Mars multiples

Date: _____

- Count to 100
- Count in steps of 2, 5 and 10

You will need:
- yellow, blue and green pencils

5

8

16

20

35

50

Teacher's notes

For each multiple of 2, children colour the planet yellow; for each multiple of 5, they colour the spaceship blue; for each multiple of 10, they colour the alien green. At the bottom of the page children write a multiple of 2 on the planet, a multiple of 5 on the spaceship and a multiple of 10 on the alien, and use the same colours as before to colour them in.

41

Date: _____

Pizza portions

Find a quarter of a shape

You will need:
- coloured pencils
- ruler

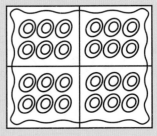

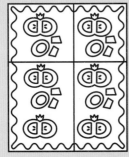

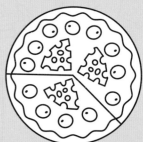

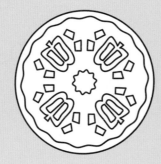

Teacher's notes

Children colour the pizzas that have been cut equally into quarters. In the last row, they colour one quarter of each pizza.

42

Date: _____

Quiver quarters

Find a quarter of a group of objects

 [ ] arrows  $\frac{1}{4}$ of [4] is [1].

 [ ] arrows  $\frac{1}{4}$ of [ ] is [ ].

 [ ] arrows  $\frac{1}{4}$ of [ ] is [ ].

 [ ] arrows  $\frac{1}{4}$ of [ ] is [ ].

Teacher's notes

Children count the arrows in each row and write the number in the box. Then they draw the arrows in the quivers so that they are shared equally between the four archers and complete the sentence.

Date: _____

Ribbon quarters

Find a quarter of a length

You will need:
- ruler
- coloured pencils

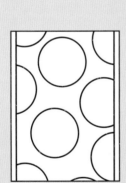

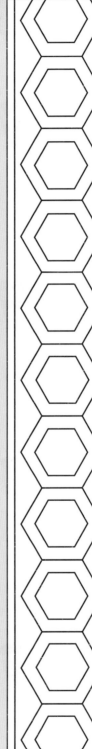

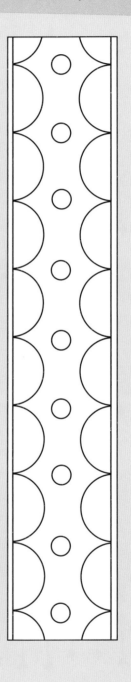

Teacher's notes

Children use a ruler to measure the length of each ribbon. They find one quarter of this length and colour one quarter of the ribbon.

Date: _____

How many pies?

Combine quarters to make one whole

☐ quarters make ☐ whole pie.

☐ quarters make ☐ whole pies.

☐ quarters make ☐ whole pies.

☐ quarters make ☐ whole pies.

Teacher's notes

Children write how many quarter pieces of pie there are on each plate. Then they draw them as whole pies and write the number of pies in the space provided to complete each statement.

Date: _____

Full or empty?

Use vocabulary related to volume and capacity

full

empty

half full

quarter full

Teacher's notes

Children look at each container and draw a line from the container to the matching label.

Date: _____

Measuring capacities

Estimate and measure capacities

You will need:
- tea cup, egg cup, plastic beaker
- spoon
- rice, pasta, water or lentils

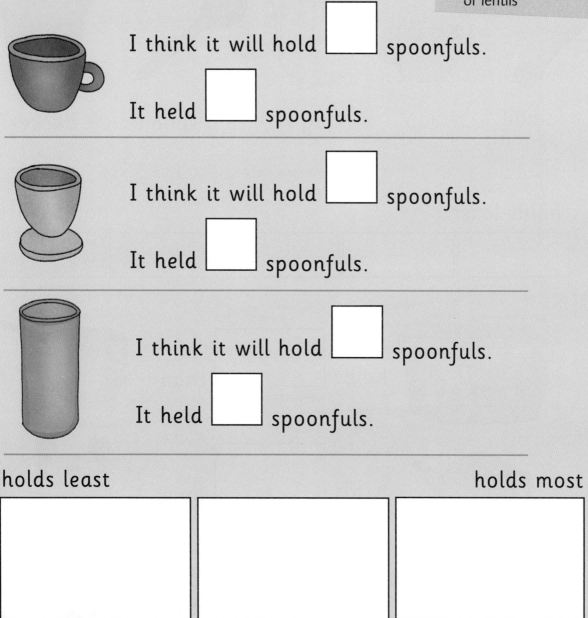

I think it will hold ☐ spoonfuls.

It held ☐ spoonfuls.

I think it will hold ☐ spoonfuls.

It held ☐ spoonfuls.

I think it will hold ☐ spoonfuls.

It held ☐ spoonfuls.

holds least   holds most

Teacher's notes

Ensure children have access to the three containers and a spoon. Using rice, pasta, water or lentils children estimate the number of spoonfuls per item. Then they measure and record the number of spoonfuls the containers hold. Finally, children draw pictures to show the containers in order of capacity.

Which measure?

Compare capacities

Date: _____

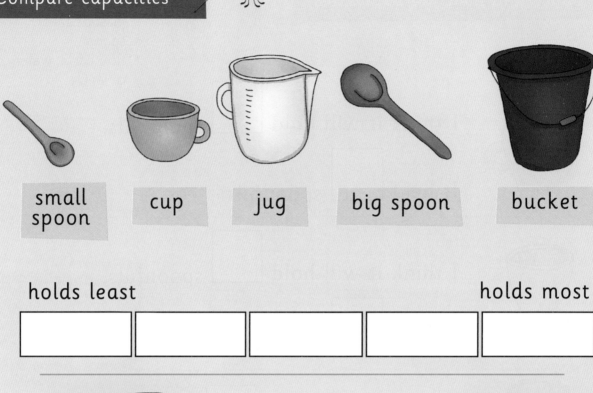

| small spoon | cup | jug | big spoon | bucket |

holds least   holds most

holds [ ] than

holds [ ] than

holds [ ] than

More, less or the same?

Compare capacities of containers with a litre

Date: _____

You will need:
- six containers of varying sizes
- litre jug
- water tray
- red and blue coloured pencils

the same as a litre

less than a litre

more than a litre

Maths facts

Number and place value

Numbers 0–20

0 1 2 3 4 5 6 7 8 9 10 11 12 13 14 15 16 17 18 19 20

Counting in steps of 2

0 2 4 6 8 10 12 14 16 18 20

1	2	3	4	5	6	7	8	9	10
11	12	13	14	15	16	17	18	19	20

Counting in steps of 5

0 5 10 15 20 25 30 35 40 45 50

1	2	3	4	5	6	7	8	9	10
11	12	13	14	15	16	17	18	19	20
21	22	23	24	25	26	27	28	29	30
31	32	33	34	35	36	37	38	39	40
41	42	43	44	45	46	47	48	49	50

Counting in steps of 10

0 10 20 30 40 50 60 70 80 90 100

1	2	3	4	5	6	7	8	9	10
11	12	13	14	15	16	17	18	19	20
21	22	23	24	25	26	27	28	29	30
31	32	33	34	35	36	37	38	39	40
41	42	43	44	45	46	47	48	49	50
51	52	53	54	55	56	57	58	59	60
61	62	63	64	65	66	67	68	69	70
71	72	73	74	75	76	77	78	79	80
81	82	83	84	85	86	87	88	89	90
91	92	93	94	95	96	97	98	99	100

Addition and subtraction facts to 5, 10 and 20

+	0	1	2	3	4	5	6	7	8	9	10
0	0	1	2	3	4	5	6	7	8	9	10
1	1	2	3	4	5	6	7	8	9	10	11
2	2	3	4	5	6	7	8	9	10	11	12
3	3	4	5	6	7	8	9	10	11	12	13
4	4	5	6	7	8	9	10	11	12	13	14
5	5	6	7	8	9	10	11	12	13	14	15
6	6	7	8	9	10	11	12	13	14	15	16
7	7	8	9	10	11	12	13	14	15	16	17
8	8	9	10	11	12	13	14	15	16	17	18
9	9	10	11	12	13	14	15	16	17	18	19
10	10	11	12	13	14	15	16	17	18	19	20

+	11	12	13	14	15	16	17	18	19	20
0	11	12	13	14	15	16	17	18	19	20
1	12	13	14	15	16	17	18	19	20	
2	13	14	15	16	17	18	19	20		
3	14	15	16	17	18	19	20			
4	15	16	17	18	19	20				
5	16	17	18	19	20					
6	17	18	19	20						
7	18	19	20							
8	19	20								
9	20									

4 o'clock

$\frac{1}{2}$ past 8

Fractions

Half: $\frac{1}{2}$

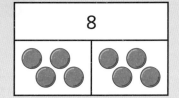

8	

Quarter: $\frac{1}{4}$

 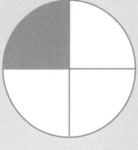

12			

2-D shapes

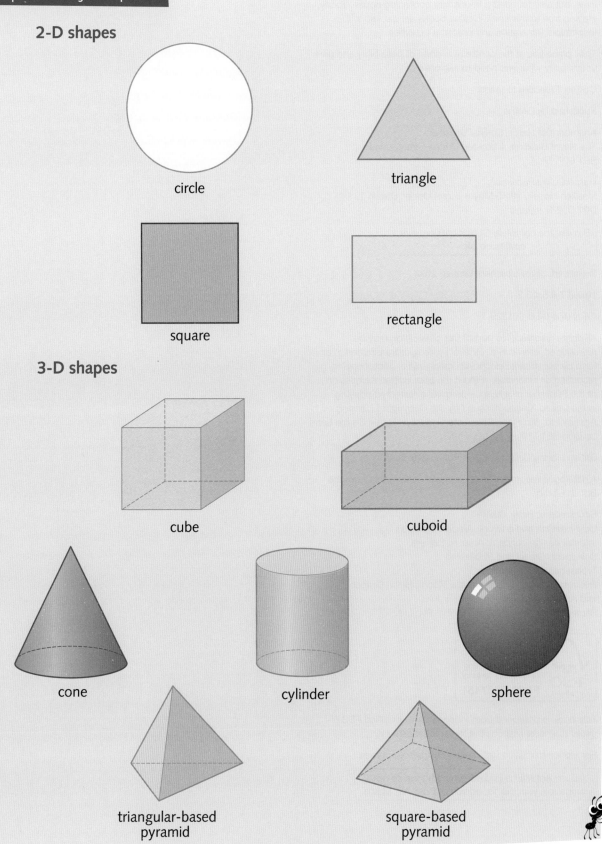

circle

triangle

square

rectangle

3-D shapes

cube

cuboid

cone

cylinder

sphere

triangular-based
pyramid

square-based
pyramid

William Collins' dream of knowledge for all began with the publication of his first book in 1819.

A self-educated mill worker, he not only enriched millions of lives, but also founded a flourishing publishing house. Today, staying true to this spirit, Collins books are packed with inspiration, innovation and practical expertise.

They place you at the centre of a world of possibility and give you exactly what you need to explore it.

Collins. Freedom to teach.

Published by Collins

An imprint of HarperCollins*Publishers*
The News Building, 1 London Bridge Street, London,
SE1 9GF, UK

HarperCollins*Publishers*
Macken House, 39/40 Mayor Street Upper, Dublin 1,
D01 C9W8, Ireland

Browse the complete Collins catalogue at
collins.co.uk

British Library Cataloguing-in-Publication Data

A catalogue record for this publication is available from the British Library.

Series editor: Peter Clarke
Cover design and artwork: Amparo Barrera
Internal design concept: Amparo Barrera
Designers: GreenGate Publishing
Typesetter: David Jimenez
Illustrators: Helen Poole, Natalia Moore, Helen Graper and Aptara
Printed in India by Multivista Global Pvt. Ltd.

MIX
Paper | Supporting
responsible forestry
FSC™ C007454

This book is produced from independently certified FSC™ paper to ensure responsible forest management.

For more information visit: harpercollins.co.uk/green

Busy Ant Maths 2nd edition components are compatible with the 1st edition of Busy Ant Maths.